YOUR KNOWLEDGE HAS VALUE

Samir Mazarweh

William Blake's "London" - An interpretation

GRIN Verlag

Bibliografische Information der Deutschen Nationalbibliothek:

Die Deutsche Bibliothek verzeichnet diese Publikation in der Deutschen National-
bibliografie; detaillierte bibliografische Daten sind im Internet über http://dnb.d-
nb.de/ abrufbar.

Imprint:

Copyright © 2010 GRIN Verlag GmbH
Druck und Bindung: Books on Demand GmbH, Norderstedt Germany
ISBN: 978-3-640-78103-4

This book at GRIN:

http://www.grin.com/en/e-book/162641/william-blake-s-london-an-interpretation

GRIN - Your knowledge has value

Der GRIN Verlag publiziert seit 1998 wissenschaftliche Arbeiten von Studenten, Hochschullehrern und anderen Akademikern als eBook und gedrucktes Buch. Die Verlagswebsite www.grin.com ist die ideale Plattform zur Veröffentlichung von Hausarbeiten, Abschlussarbeiten, wissenschaftlichen Aufsätzen, Dissertationen und Fachbüchern.

Visit us on the internet:

http://www.grin.com/

http://www.facebook.com/grincom

http://www.twitter.com/grin_com

Ruprecht Karls-Universität Heidelberg

Anglistic Department
PS I Introduction to City Poetry: London
WS 09/10

William Blake´s

"London"

Contents

Introduction

This paper tries to provide an insight into the analysis of 18th century author William Blake's poem `London'.

Comments from Blake experts like the following from Edward Thompson make this task appear easy. He said: "`London' is among the most lucid and instantly available of the *Songs of Experience*."[1] On the one hand I agree to this statement. The poem itself is easy to understand, not much background information about the author's life, his visions, and his complete works is required to grasp the message. However, an analysis has to provide more than just make the message of a poem understandable. It should inter alia deal with the circumstances the author lived in, the work of which the poem is part of, and last but not least, the stylistic devices and linguistic images used in this piece of art.

In the case of `London', this has been done by professionals many times, a fact leading us to another important point that makes the task appear easier than it actually is: The mass of biographies, comments, analyses, and criticisms that have been written about Blake and his works. The advantage is obvious: Every line of `London' has been discussed and commented on, and all that must be done is find adequate information. At the same time this amount of literature presents many different approaches to analyse the poem; too many to introduce them in a ten-page paper. Hence, this assignment tries to show a few aspects only: After introducing the author and the `Songs of Innocence and of Experience' very briefly, it follows a short summary of the poem and an overview of the stylistic devices. The sixth chapter is the analysis itself, focusing on the social criticism of the poem, while only dealing with the "very complex relations between reading, and hearing, and seeing"[2] superficially.

---

1 E.P. Thompson, *Witness against the beast: William Blake and the moral law.* (Cambridge: Cambridge University Press, 1994) p. 174.
2 Gavin Edwards, *Mind forg'd manacles: A Contribution to the Discussion of Blake's London.* (1979) p. 87.

1. Biography

William Blake was born on 28th November 1757 in London as third of seven children of a hosier and bargainer. He grew up as part of London´s lower middle-class, and as such it was normal that he used to help his father in his business dealings. This is one of the reasons why he did not become a good pupil, but hardly learned how to read and write. His parents soon recognised that William had interests other than conventional school, and hence they supported his motivation to become an artist by sending him to a special drawing school. This, of course, influenced his whole life and constituted the starting point of his career as a painter. The fact that he became an engraver later made him introduce his profession into his passion, and a product of this combination seems to be his invention of relief etching, a reversal of the method of etching. Another important thing to mention is an unusualness in his life: Blake claimed to see angels, daemons, and ghosts around him. He even stated to be able to have conversations with them, and throughout his life he never changed his mind about this. This led many of his contemporaries to think that he is mentally ill. Blake´s rude attacks on Christianity, or more precise, on the Church of England contributed to this attitude. This must not be understood as him being not religious. In fact it seems that he was very religious and designed his own religion and myths, but could not get along with the views the Church held. In contrast to his contemporaries, his wife, Catherine Boucher, whom he married in 1782 obviously stuck by him. It is said that their marriage was very happy, although they had no children, and, as a result of the attitude adopted towards him and his works, lived in poverty for years. She helped him produce his paintings, and he taught her to read and write. It was together with her that Blake left London for the first and last time in his life. They moved to Felpham, a village near to Portsmouth, in 1800 and stayed their for three years, after which they returned to the capital. On 12th August 1827, four years before his wife, William Blake died in London.[3]

---

3   http://www.william-blake.de/cv.php, http://www.online-literature.com/blake/,
    http://en.wikipedia.org/wiki/William_Blake, http://www.poets.org/poet.php/prmPID/116 (25.02.10).

2. The Songs

The `Songs of Innocence and of Experience: Shewing the two Contrary Sides of the Human Soul´ are a series of poems divided in two books. Every poem goes along with an illustration. The first book, the `Songs of Innocence´ was first printed in 1789, and the second book, the `Songs of Experience´, in 1793. They were published together in the year 1794 and have built one piece since then, which contains of 45 poems, 19 in the first and 26 in the second book. Blake's subtitle is probably the best way to describe the work: The two books show the two contrary sides of the human soul. `The Songs of Innocence´ convey a positive, light-hearted atmosphere; since the poems´ titles speak for themselves there is no need for an extensive description: `The Lamb´, `The Blossom´, `Laughing Song´, and `Infant´s Joy´ are some examples. `The Songs of Experience´ are in total contrast to the first book.[4] A dark and depressing atmosphere is predominant. The innocence of the child is lost and has made room for the grown-up´s experience.

Several poems have a counterpart in the other book, making it possible to compare them directly. Not so `London´, which is part of the `Songs of Experience´.

3. `London´

I wander thro' each charter'd street,
Near where the charter'd Thames does flow,
And mark in every face I meet
Marks of weakness, marks of woe.

In every cry of every Man,
In every Infant's cry of fear,
In every voice, in every ban,
The mind-forg'd manacles I hear.

How the Chimney-sweeper's cry
Every black'ning Church appals;
And the hapless Soldier's sigh
Runs in blood down Palace walls.

But most thro' midnight streets I hear
How the youthful Harlot's curse
Blasts the new born Infant's tear,
And blights with plagues the Marriage hearse.[5]

---

4   e.g. the poems´ titles: `The Tyger´ (in contrast to `The Lamb´), The `Sick Rose´ (in contrast to `The Blossom´), etc.
5   cf. the copy in: Gardner, Stanley. *The Tyger, the lamb, and the terrible desart.* (Cranbury: Fairleigh Dickinson University Press, 1998.)

4. Summary

A nameless first-person narrator walks through the streets of London and observes the condition of the city and its inhabitants. He recognises that the streets and even the river are chartered. The speaker notices hardship and sorrow everywhere he goes: Marks of weakness in the people´s faces, cries of children and grown ups likewise, the sigh of a soldier, the curse of a prostitute. Institutions like the *Church* and the *Palace* are connected with these hardships. A dark and negative atmosphere is omnipresent.

5. Stylistic Devices

The poem contains of sixteen lines divided into four stanzas with four lines each. The meter in the four quatrains is mostly an iambic tetrameter. Exceptions are lines 4, 9 to 12, 14, and 15. In these lines the meter is trochaic. The rhyme scheme is an alternate rhyme with full, masculine rhymes. Another typical feature of the poem is the Enjambment found in lines 3 to 4, 9 to 10, 11 to 12, 13 to 14, and 14 to 15. However, the most striking stylistic device used by Blake is the repetition. He makes use of word repetitions, e.g. *charter´d* in lines 1 and 2, *cry* in lines 5, 6, and 9, or *infant* in lines 6 and 15. Besides that, Blake repeats phrases in the beginning of successive lines (Anaphora) like *in every* in lines 5, 6, and 7. Furthermore a figura etymologica can be found in lines 3 and 4: The verb *mark* is repeated and modified to the noun *marks*. There are repetitions on the letter level, e.g. an Alliteration in line eleven: *soldier´s sigh,* or the frequent use of certain letters like the *b* in the last five lines of the poem. The poet shows the reader his skills by combining a repetition on the word and on the letter level: The word *hear* is not only repeated in lines 8 and 13, but also in the initial letters of the third stanza. When using the word ´repetition´ in the paper, repetitions on the phrase, the word, and the letter level are meant.

The devices are referred to in chapter 6 in more detail and integrated in the interpretation, hence not every phenomenon is mentioned here.

6. Analysis

In the following the poem is analysed verse by verse. My personal interpretation, the professionals' comments, and the connection to the stylistic features introduced in chapter 5 are dealt with at the same time to guarantee an easy reading. Splitting the three parts into three chapters would mean that the reader has to jump from chapter to chapter every time a reference is made.

I wander thro' each charter'd street. The narrator starts his walk through the streets. Since the poem starts with the personal pronoun *I*, it seems natural to begin the analysis with it. The attention is immediately drawn to the lyrical I to show that it is its personal perspective that this poem is written from. The speaker wanders, marks, and hears, and he tells the reader what he sees, or, what he wants the reader to notice. Adams calls the speaker "an indignant critic"[6] who "is clearly exploring the city."[7] No doubt the speaker is a straight critic, since he does not hesitate to name the problems and catastrophes present in the city. However, he seems not to be exploring the city but to know it very well, and hence he is able to present a profound result of his walk. The use of the verb *wander* hints at the fact that the speaker does not have a target, but it can not be inferred that he is a stranger, who explores the city.

The author of the poem should not be mixed up with the lyrical I, however it is not hard to imagine William Blake walking through London making the same statements the speaker does.

The most controversial word in the first line is *charter'd*. The speaker sees the streets chartered as well as the river. The verb could theoretically have several different meanings like founded, privileged, protected, licensed, or hired.[8] Since the East India Company, the largest company known on the Thames, renewed its charter for twenty years in the time Blake wrote his poem, it becomes clear that *charter'd* is connected to economy and trading here[9]. Blake, grown up in the lower middle-class, understands the problem connected to this renewal: Ordinary people, part of smaller companies or having smaller companies themselves, are too weak to compete with large companies

---

6   Hazard Adams, *William Blake a reading of the shorter poems*. (Seattle: University of Washington
            Press, 1963) p. 276.
7   ibid. p. 277.
8   *The Oxford English Dictionary.* Volume II C. (Oxford: Oxford University Press, 1933).
9   cf. E.P. Thompson, *Witness against the beast.* (Cambridge: Cambridge University Press, 1994) p. 176.

like the East India and are therefore facing hard times. By choosing this word Blake furthermore emphasises that when streets or even rivers are hired to a few people, many other people are excluded[10]; in his opinion this is unjust. In Blake's first draft the word *dirty* appeared instead of *charter'd*. This points to the thesis that he wanted *charter'd* to be understood in the most negative way possible[11].

Near where the charter'd Thames does flow. The narrator states that even London's river is hired. The repetition of *charter'd* in the second line adds to the feeling of the whole city being hired. By naming the river Thames in the second line, the speaker makes it clear for the reader through which city he is walking, and by stating that he is walking *near* the river, the reader can even imagine where in London the speaker is. This leads to an identification with the speaker and a sense of being close to him. The flow of a river is usually associated with freedom, however by combining it with the verb *charter'd* the opposite feeling is emphasised.

And mark in every face I meet Marks of weakness, marks of woe. The people seen by the narrator are unhappy and sick. Since he is not examining the Londoners but just looking at them, the marks of weakness and woe must be clearly visible signs of affliction and sickness.[12] The word *every* evokes the feeling that every single man the speaker sees, without exceptions, is weak or suffering. This sentence is a kind of introduction of the negative atmosphere connected to the whole poem, further intensified through the use of *weakness* and *woe*, which are clearly negatively connoted. The two words are connected to each other by an alliteration and by being part of an anaphora. Added to the other repetitions, an agglomeration of at least six repetitions[13] are found in the first stanza, which causes a dismal and monotonous feeling and hence further intensifies the negative atmosphere.

In every cry of every Man. Again, the use of the word *every* indicates that no exceptions are found, and the repetition of it in lines 5, 6, and 7 for five times generates a feeling of desperation.

In every Infant's cry of fear. Not only the men are crying, but also the children. Here the way of crying is defined more precisely. The children are crying of fear, however the reason of their fear is not clear.

---

10 cf. ibid. p. 177.
11 cf. ibid. p.175.
12 http://21stcenturysocialism.com/article/william_blakes_london_01594.html (01.03.10).
13 phrase repetitions: (anaphora) *Marks of* in line 4. word repetitions: *I* in line 1 and 3, *charter'd* in line 1 and 2, *mark* in line 3 and 4. letter repetitions: (alliterations) *mark* and *meet* in line 3, *weakness* and *woe* in line 4.

In every voice, in every ban. The mind-forged manacles are not only heard in every cry, but also in every ban, and to make it as general as possible: in every voice. Simon Korner's comment on the first three lines of the second stanza is as simple as precise: "No-one is immune."[14] The mind-forged manacles can be heard everywhere.

The mind-forg'd manacles I hear. What is meant with the mind-forged manacles? Manacles are chains or handcuffs, hence mind-forged manacles must be chains manufactured by someone's mind. Perhaps Blake hints at the hopeless situation of the people described in lines 5 to 7. Their minds create manacles, since they do not even hope to be able to change their living conditions. The poverty, the wide-spread illnesses, the social injustice are a too heavy burden. "The Earth is chained as much by its own psychological predisposition as by social injustice."[15] On the other hand this wording could be an allusion to the manacles forced on the people by the rulers i.e. the king. A look at Blake's first draft, in which he wrote *the german forgd links I hear,*[16] supports this view. David Erdman as well as E.P. Thompson[17] state that the poet referred to the Hanoverian monarchy and especially George III. of the United Kingdom, who reigned Great Britain from 1760 – 1820.[18] It was said about him that he wanted to use Hanoverian troops against British reformers, which must have been a thorn in Blake's flesh to say the least. Besides that, George III. was king during the time of the American Revolutionary War, and "is often accused of obstinately trying to keep Great Britain at war with the revolutionaries in America"[19], which probably caused Blake to criticise him in 'London'. Independently, the wording *mind-forg'd manacles* gives a more general meaning and thus is a more general criticism.

Most eye-catching is Blake's choice to use the verb *hear* in this line and this context. It is repeated three times throughout the poem: In lines 8 and 13, and also in the initial letters of the third stanza, which additionally emphasises the importance of the word. However, the use in line 13 is easily comprehensible, and the use in the initial letters is a kind of play with the language, while the use in line 8 does not become clear in a first reading. It is important to understand that the manacles are not really heard, in fact there

14 http://21stcenturysocialism.com/article/william_blakes_london_01594.html (01.03.10).
15 Wolf Mankowitz, *The Songs of Experience.* (London: Macmillan, 1970) p. 132.
16 cf. V. Doyno, *Blake's Revision of London.* p.58.
17 cf. E.P. Thompson, *Witness against the Beast.* p. 183.
18
    http://www.royal.gov.uk/HistoryoftheMonarchy/KingsandQueensoftheUnitedKingdom/TheHano verians/GeorgeIII.aspx (01.03.10).
19 http://en.wikipedia.org/wiki/George_III_of_the_United_Kingdom#American_Revolutionary_War (03.03.10).

is something in the voices of the people that reminds the speaker of the mind-forged manacles. Thompson interprets the phenomenon as follows: "(...) the passage from sight to sound has an effect of reducing the sense of distance or of the alienation of the observer from his object (...)"[20] The speaker solely observes in the first stanza. While it is not possible to see many different things at one time, it is possible to hear many things at the same time, which is the case here.[21] After having seen the streets, then the Thames, then the faces the speaker hears every cry, voice, and ban simultaneously and transports this experience to the reader. This gives the reader an intensified connection to the situation. So the function of the verb *hear* in this context is to modify the atmosphere of the poem; it is still negative, but the reader is drawn closer to it.

Stanzas three and four contain several examples of social grievance, which, after bringing him close to the event, hit the reader with full strength: "The interdependent misery of the inhabitants of this London is most forcefully expressed in the poem's concluding stanza."[22]

How the Chimney-sweeper's cry Every black'ning Church appals; The Chimney sweeper is an example for injustice and immoral treatment of the weaker parts of society. Often small children, not older than 5 years, were forced to carry out this hard and harmful work because they were able to enter the chimneys and clean them from inside. Many of them died before entering adulthood. In the year 1788 the `Act for the Better Regulation of Chimney Sweepers and their Apprentices´ was passed, saying that chimney sweepers had to be eight years old (!) at least.[23] It took several decades however since this and similar acts were enforced. In the time when William Blake wrote `London´, nobody really cared about these children and correspondingly miserable was their situation.[24] The chimney sweeper's cry is heard by the speaker, but ignored by the Church, which is personified in this verse and thereby concretised. It is clearly heard by it, since it is appalled by the sound, but the responsible persons do not react. The Church should be a benevolent institution standing against injustice and defending the children's rights; however it does not. Furthermore the Church is attributed with the verb *black'ning,* casting an even worse light on it. On the one hand

---

20 E.P. Thompson, *London* (Cambridge: Cambridge University Press, 1978) p. 18.
21 cf. ibid. p. 18.
22 Wolf Mankowitz, *The Songs of Experience* (London: Macmillan, 1970) p. 132.
23 http://www.parliament.uk/about/livingheritage/transformingsociety/19thcentury/keydates.cfm (09.03.10).
24 Blake refers two the children's destiny in two poems, one in the `Songs of Innocence´ and one in the `Songs of Experience´.

black'ning carries the meaning of the church walls becoming blacker and blacker. This is probably a hint to the proceeding industrialization: The more factories are built, the more smoke and grime is blown into the air, polluting it and constituting a health risk for the people. On the other hand it has a metaphorical meaning: Black is the colour of grief and sorrow[25], and in this context also of guilt and somewhat of evilness. This view is supported by the fact that line 10 was changed by Blake from *Blackens oer the churches walls*[26] to *Every black'ning Church appals*. In the first draft the Church is shown as passive and accordingly not involved, maybe not even guilty, while in the final version the Church is aware and hence responsible.[27] E.P. Thompson comments on this line:

> By revising the line Blake has simply tightened up the strings of his indignation by another notch. (...) the adjective `blackning' visually attaching to the Church complicity in the brutal exploitation of young childhood along with the wider consequences of the smoke of expanding commerce.[28]

And the hapless Soldier's sigh Runs in blood down Palace walls. The soldier is nothing but a victim of the system he himself is part of. He is not convinced of the idea he is fighting and dying for, but he has no choice: George III., the head of the ruling class and hence the personified *Palace walls*, sent troops to America to fight the revolutionaries there, and was also at war with the French revolutionaries, so the army had to fight. David Erdman chooses another approach when saying that the hapless soldiers are the British citizens, who are urged to defend themselves against the increasing number of Hanoverian mercenaries in Britain.[29] Anyway, Blake directly criticizes the royalty and its unjustifiable handling of the army. He further underlines this accusation by using a synaesthesia binding the *Soldier's sigh* and the *Palace walls* together closely. The *blood* could be the soldier's, flushing out of the wounds he suffered in one of the battles. It is running down the Palace walls as a complaint, since he did not want to fight this battle. Again, David Erdman understands this line differently. For him, it records the citizens' "inclination (...) to turn from grumbling to mutiny".[30] This inclination was expressed by

---

25 at least in catholic tradition.
26 cf. V. Doyno, *Blake's revision of London.* p. 58.
27 cf. E.P. Thompson, *London.* p. 16.
28 E.P. Thompson, *London.* p. 16.
29 David V. Erdman, *Infinite London* (New Jersey: Prentice-Hall, 1969) p. 56.
30 ibid. p. 56.

slogans like "No king!", written on the walls of the Privy Garden.[31]

After totally fading out the lyrical I in the third stanza, it is reintroduced in line 13, sharing another discovery with the reader.

But most thro' midnight streets I hear. Line 13 is a kind of announcement given by the speaker: "What I have described thus far is not the full horror of London."[32] This increases the readers' suspense. Also remarkable is the description *midnight streets.* The day has turned to night; although it is not mentioned that it was daytime in the first three stanzas this conclusion has to be made. How else could the speaker see all the things he describes?[33] The darkness surrounds the whole world now, thereby building the completion of the negative atmosphere.

How the youthful Harlot's curse Blasts the new born Infant's tear, And blights with plagues the Marriage hearse. In the last three lines Blake alludes to another defect in London's society, namely the wide-spread prostitution[34]. Again young members of the community are abused. Bachelors have intercourse with the young harlots, are infected with venereal diseases, *the Harlot's curse*, and pass it on to their wives after the marriage. As a consequence, the women infect the newborns with these illnesses. By this means the marriage car becomes a hearse.

The combination of *marriage* and *hearse* is an example of how the author manages to transform the few words with positive connotations[35] into phrases with negative connotations.

The accumulation of the letter *b* in the fourth stanza adds to the negative atmosphere, particularly because it is, in the 16 lines, almost exclusively used as initial letter of words with negative connotations.[36]

Another time, the speaker hears something that usually can not be heard. It is not the *curse* he hears, but the *blast* and the *blighting.* This synaesthesia establishes a stylistic connection between the prostitute, the infant, and the spouses and has its climax in the poem's last word *hearse,* which is a combination of hear and see.

---

31 cf. ibid. p. 56.
32 http://www.multimedialibrary.com/Articles/kazin/alfredblake.asp (10.03.10).
33 Especially marks of weakness in a man's face can hardly be recognized in the darkness.
34 It is said that there were thousands of prostitutes in London in the late 1790's. According to the Independent, in 1839 there were an estimated 80,000 prostitutes among 2 million inhabitants. (http://www.independent.co.uk/life-style/love-sex/culture-of-love/a-brief-cultural-history-of-sex-938527.html (10.03.10)).
35 *infant* in l. 6 and l. 15, *youthful* in l. 14., and *marriage* in l.16.
36 *ban, black'ning, blood, blasts, blights.* Note the increase of b-words throughout the poem (zero in the first, one in the second, two in the third, and four in the fourth stanza).

Conclusion

As mentioned in the Introduction, there are several different approaches to this poem, like interpreting `London´ in regard to the Bible, which would give a totally different outcome to this paper.

In the above it was tried to show that `London´ is sociocritical. Both the ruling and the ruled class are criticised. The speaker sees different kinds of manacles everywhere in the city. The chimney sweeper, the soldier, the harlot – all of them have manacles on. Some have put them on themselves, others got them put on by the society as a whole or by certain institutions. These manacles are an indication for the speaker that the society is sick, which then again makes the speaker suffer. A hopeless and dismal atmosphere mirrored by the choice of words and images is the result.

William Blake recognised this hopeless condition as he proves with the poem. However, the poem also proves that he could not or did not want to present a way out of the situation. As the author states in the title of the Songs, his intention is to show how the human soul is, which he did successfully in `London´.

Bibliography

Primary sources

Gardner, Stanley. *The Tyger, the lamb, and the terrible desart: Songs of innocence and of experience in its time and circumstance: including facsimiles of two copies.* Cranbury: Fairleigh Dickinson University Press, 1998.

Secondary sources

Ackroyd, Peter. *Blake.* London: Sinclair-Stevenson, 1995.

Adams, Hazard. *William Blake: a reading of the shorter poems.* Seattle: University of Washington Press, 1963.

Beer, John B. *William Blake – a literary life.* New York: Palgrave Macmillan, 2005.

Bindman, David. *Mind-forg'd manacles: William Blake and slavery.* London: The Hayward Gallery Publishing, 2007.

Damon, S. Foster. A Blake dictionary: *The ideas and Symbols of William Blake.* Rhode Island: Brown University Press, 1965.

Digby, George Wingfield. *Symbol and Image in William Blake.* Oxford: Oxford University Press, 1957.

Doyno, V. "Blake's revision of `London'." *Essays in Criticism* 24.1 (1972): 58-63.

Edwards, Gavin. "Mind forg'd manacles: A Contribution to the Discussion of Blake's `London'." *Literature and History* 5.1 (1979): p. 87 – 105.

Erdman, David V. *Blake: Prophet against Empire: A Poet's Interpretation of the History of his own Times.* New Jersey: Princeton University Press, 1954.

Erdman, David V. "Infinite London." *Twentieth Century Interpretations of Songs of Innocence and of Experience.* Ed. Morton D. Paley. New Jersey: Prentice-Hall, 1969. 49 – 57.

Hirsch, E.D.,jr. *Innocence and Experience: an introduction to Blake.* New Haven: Yale University Press, 1964.

Larrissy, Edward. *William Blake.* Ed. Terry Eagleton. Oxford: Blackwell, 1985.

Lindsay, David W. *Blake: Songs of Innocence and Experience.* London: Macmillan, 1989.

Mankowitz, Wolf. "The Songs of Experience." *William Blake: Songs of Innocence and Experience.* Ed. Margaret Bottrall. London: Macmillan, 1970. 123 – 135.

Thompson, E.P. *Witness against the beast: William Blake and the moral law.* Cambridge: Cambridge University Press, 1994.

Thompson, E.P. "London." *Interpreting Blake*. Ed. Michael Phillips. Cambridge: Cambridge University Press, 1978. 5 – 31.

Rix, Robert. *William Blake and the cultures of radical Christianity*. Hampshire: Ashgate Publishing Limited, 2007.

Williams, Nicholas M. *Ideology and Utopia in the poetry of William Blake*. Cambridge: Cambridge University Press, 1998.

Dictionary:

The Oxford English Dictionary. Volume II C. Oxford: Oxford University Press, 1933.

Internet:

http://www.william-blake.de/cv.php (25.02.10)

http://www.online-literature.com/blake/ (25.02.10)

http://en.wikipedia.org/wiki/William_Blake (25.02.10)

http://www.poets.org/poet.php/prmPID/116 (25.02.10)

http://eic.oxfordjournals.org/cgi/reprint/XXII/1/58 (01.03.10)

http://21stcenturysocialism.com/article/william_blakes_london_01594.html (01.03.10)

http://www.independent.co.uk/life-style/love-sex/culture-of-love/a-brief-cultural-history-of-sex-938527.html (10.03.10)

http://www.multimedialibrary.com/Articles/kazin/alfredblake.asp (10.03.10)